Blessings

Pursuit of Peace

By Ron Camerrer

Pursuit of Peace

By Ron Camerrer
Fort Collins, Colorado

ISBN-13: 978-1539490364
ISBN-10: 153949036X

Forward

Years ago, a man in my businessmen's Bible study asked me a key question. "What is the most pressing problem that people face?" My response was immediate, "Stress, worry, and anxiety." The computer industry at the time had a name for this response– FUD – Fear, Uncertainty, and Doubt.

The man who asked the question was Ron Camerrer. A few months later he had written a series of booklets entitled the "Pursuit of Peace." Those booklets became a book and Ron became known as the "Pursuit of Peace" guy.

Now many years later, I have encouraged Ron to write the second edition of "Pursuit of Peace," because of two things; with most everybody I meet, stress and worry are more prevalent than ever. Ron has gained incredible wisdom over the years about the pursuit of peace. Not only does Ron have subject matter wisdom, his personal life demonstrates that a man (or woman) can have peace regardless of circumstances.

Peace is not something that happens to us. It is a choice we proactively make. In the pages following, Ron will lay out a path for you on how you can have peace, regardless of the circumstances you face. You will hear from Ron about some simple action steps (Pursuit) that you can take.

I have been blessed to watch Ron and learn from him. As a result, I can honestly say that, "I have peace." True peace comes from the Lord and Ron has set the example. Please enjoy the wisdom and insight that follows from my friend Ron Camerrer.

Ken Hoornbeek

Hospital

Two times now, I had been to the hospital. Two times, the heart surgery had been canceled. Now I had to wait almost another week. I had lots of time to ponder, worry, and think about what was going to happen. For one of the medicines I had to take, I had to use a needle by myself to inject the medication into my stomach. Was I scared? Absolutely!

During this final week prior to surgery, I had time to slow down. When I look back, I realize these waiting periods were what I needed. I had an opportunity to calm down, pray, and draw closer to God.

Even though I was tremendously scared, I talked to God, every day. I also spent time with my youngest daughter, who lived over in the next town. My other daughter came in later from out-of-state. Through it all, I maintained my daily Bible reading pattern every morning.

On Thursday evening prior to the Friday morning surgery, I checked in to the hospital.

My son-in-law came to me in the hospital and asked if I had a will.

"No, I don't."

"I know it's difficult to talk about... well, you probably really need to do this, for everyone's sake."

That's when I knew I was facing head-on with death. Later I wrote a couple of paragraphs on a sheet of notebook paper and gave it to my daughter. I had no assets to bequeath. However, I put in one statement concerning where I would end up if I didn't make it through surgery.

I wrote, "I want everyone to know that Papa will be up in heaven and that, even up there, I would be an angel watching over my family and grandkids." I wanted my family to know without a doubt that I was a Christian. I wanted them to think about following me to heaven.

I knew there would be a lot of pain with the heart surgery. I prayed to God to help me with the pain.

God answered. I went through the double bypass surgery with virtually no pain! A compulsory peace encompassed my whole spiritual and physical body. Despite the circumstances, I basked in true peace.

You do not have to go through a heart operation to find peace. I was at peace before and after the operation. Despite all the obstacles, peace had come and enveloped me, even on the day after the surgery.

Left-Handed Glove

A surprising victory in my life...

It's very easy to become discouraged when you are just barely getting by. There is no use to complain about lack of money, because complaining doesn't get you anywhere. You learn to get by with what you have. I always, and still do, base my spending on the fact that, "I can out-crawl anybody (unless they were worse off than me.)"

It was icy cold in the winter in the middle of January. I could barely scrape the ice off my windshield and windows of my Jeep Cherokee. I was using my right hand because a few months ago, I lost my left-hand glove... somewhere. Money was barely existent. I could hardly afford a cup of coffee. Every purchase, and I mean every purchase, had to have a great deal of deliberation on my part. I was accustomed to having no money. My decisions were pretty much all laid out for me.

In the parking lot of the apartment house where I lived, the Jeep heater took a while to warm up. My body was shuddering from the cold. It must have been around five degrees outside. Inside my Jeep, it felt like it was about ten degrees below zero.

I start off my mornings with a prayer. I implored God to help me get enough money so I could buy a pair of gloves. Guess what?

God didn't answer my specific prayer!

That morning, as I headed down the street behind a snowplow, I spotted something on the edge of the freshly plowed snow. There was no traffic. For some reason, I stopped in the middle of the street. I put my Jeep in reverse. When I got up to the object, I climbed out of my Jeep and picked it up.

It was an old greasy work glove! I tried it on! Sure enough, it was a left-handed glove. I now had gloves for all my icy fingers.

I used that mismatched pair of gloves for the rest of that winter.

God didn't give me the new gloves I asked for... but he did give me what I needed.

Do I believe in prayer? "Yes, I do." The more I make a habit to pray, the more opportunities I give to God to answer my prayers.

Before the next winter, I finally purchased a new warm pair of gloves. I now have a warm pair of gloves for each of my coats. I have never forgotten praying and then finding that left-handed glove in the snow behind the snowplow.

Luke 12: 29-31
"And do not set your heart on what you will eat or drink; do not worry about it. For the pagan world runs after all such things, and your Father knows you need them. But seek ye first his kingdom, and all these things will be given to you as well."

John 14:27
"Peace I leave with you; my peace I give you. I do not give to you as the world gives. Do not let your hearts be troubled and do not be afraid."

Living As If You Were Rich

One Saturday morning, a six year old boy asked his father, "Daddy, what does it mean to be rich?"

The boy's father thought for a moment on how to answer his son's question.

"Well... if you are rich, you live in a big house... and you have so much money that you can buy anything you want."

"I have money in my piggy bank. Are we rich, Daddy?"

"Well, no, son. We aren't rich. We live in a nice house and we work hard for whatever we get, so we do just fine."

The little boy appeared as if in deep thought. Then he ran into the kitchen where his mother was just taking out hot biscuits from the oven. He repeated his question.

"Mommy, are we rich?"

The mother grabbed the little boy into her arms and said, "Yes, we are rich. We have you don't we?"

The little boy pondered and then replied, "I am glad we are rich. It makes me feel good inside. Can you take me to the store?"

"Why do you want to go to the store?"

"I want to buy you and Daddy something with my money in my piggy bank."

I still practice peace and faith every day. I am known as a "man of peace." You can also be a "man or woman of peace."

I encourage you to step out in faith and follow the peace principles laid out in this book.

I am just a man who has faced stress head-on and made it through the challenges and setbacks. This is the story of my journey. Perhaps these principles will help you on your journey to peace. Yes, you can decide to begin having a new life without stress! You can become an overcomer! It's OK to become peaceful.

After my double bypass heart surgery, at the cardiologist's office when I took the first treadmill test, I asked the attending nurse, "How close was I to dying?"

She pondered on how to respond.

"Let's just say you are a very lucky man."

Wait to Worry

Have you ever worried about something? I'm sure you have. This is the story how I began overcoming worry.

I was having a very discouraging time. My spirit was so low that I felt like a spider crawling along on a wood floor. I felt like all I wanted to do was to go hide somewhere.

I was sitting in a grocery store delicatessen. My friend, Jay, came in. We often had morning coffee together. Jay listened to all my woes.

He told me about a TV pastor's sermon that he had heard yesterday. Jay said the pastor used this phrase in his message, "Wait to worry."

Sinking into my soul, somehow Jay's words comforted me. I remember that particular day because on that day, I began changing my thinking.

Have you ever considered sharing some of your struggles with a good friend? Of course this takes courage. For me, it was a major step on the trail of finding peace.

As I said, my thinking changed. I made a decision that I was going to follow that Pastor's sermon. I didn't know, "how to wait to worry," but I took a small step forward, that turned into a giant leap.

My turn-around catapulted me into trusting something other than my own thoughts of helplessness and despair.

I made a choice to not worry. I still had plenty to worry about, but the worry didn't bother me anymore. This was one of the first major steps I took to invigorate my comeback trail.

Can you actually worry about something that hasn't happened yet? This is the essence of worry, however it's wise to note that, "Every worry hasn't happened yet."

Every worry is "fear in action." By worrying, can you effect a change in an event or a situation?

"No!" Then why worry about it?

This Bible Verse below rings true for me. Perhaps it will make an encouraging difference for you, too.

Matthew 6: 25-27

"Therefore I tell you, do not worry about your life, what you will eat or drink, or about your body, what you will wear. Is not life more important than clothes? Look at the birds of the air; they do not sow or reap or store away in barns, and yet your heavenly Father feeds them. Are you not much more valuable than they? Who of you by worrying can add a single hour to his life?"

A good plan...

At the height of my discouraging times, I asked my good friend, Nathan, how he handled the worry problems with his job. He was a real estate salesman. Here was his written reply:

You are sitting there, worried about all the pressures of life. They seem overwhelming, almost too much. You want to get a handle on it all, get to work improving those areas of your life that seem out of control. You sit there looking at the wall, where to begin? It is like standing in a pitch-dark room. Do you turn, walk, or sit down? It seems so overwhelming you can't start.

It is time to make a step-by-step of your life that you CAN follow. Start with what you want to change, what you want to accomplish.

No matter how big or small the change is, write it down, one accomplishment per page. Now look at that first page. What can you do to take that first step towards that goal? What do you need to take that first step? List each of these under the step. Keep listing steps until you reach the point where you can take that step... now.

Have you ever considered writing down a goal plan for your life? I found that the goal plan I was encouraged to write down, literally guided me onto the path of peace. I wrote these thoughts on paper so that I could review them often. What are your thoughts and inner desires for true and real peace?

My plan I wrote down...

My overall goal is to remove all stress from my life and replace with peace, contentment, and happiness...every day. I want to be a kid again and I will achieve that status through my kids and my grandkids, especially my grandkids.

Every business thing I do will be done by concentrating on getting the most out of every effort, in the shortest amount of time. I will live on effectiveness and gain more free time all of the time.

I propose living in happiness, peace, and harmony the rest of my life.

The peaceful life...

At first, the peaceful life may take a lot of effort on your part, but I have found the results are absolutely worth it!

When you are seeking peace, you will discover that true peace begins and ends with belief and faith in God.

Can you become an encourager to others? Yes.

Can you deliberately seek peace in each situation you encounter? Yes.

Remember, peace is a choice, not an event.

My first task tomorrow is to continue pursuing peace. I make it a daily habit to engage in prayer before I start the day. For you and me, that's the very first accomplishment for the day. No matter what happens, you can start off the day with peace. God will allow you to have as much peace as you want. You do have to ask.

It's OK to have a good day!

Faith Principle:

God will take care of what you need, even when you don't know what you need.

Thinking

I was sitting on a rock up in a mountain subdivision called Glacier View Meadows. Have you ever intentionally driven to a beautiful quiet place for the express purpose of "thinking things through?" You might want to try it. In the midst of nature, your mind can organize and sift through the problems you might be facing.

I was worried about a particular part time job I had been offered. My previous part time job had been eliminated. Now, I had no job at all. I came up specifically to pray to God about whether or not to take on the new job.

After about ten minutes of sitting there quietly in the summer breeze, a strident voice from over my left shoulder distinctly said, "Go get your job!"

I immediately got back in my jeep and headed back to the city. Within a week, my new part time job was paying me triple what I had been making at the old part time job. I also was now doing what I always wanted to do. I had always wanted to be a teacher. The new part time job was teaching at a real estate licensing school.

By intentionally placing myself in a peaceful environment, I heard directly from God. The voice, I think, was an angel telling me what to do.

Accept the real fact that it is possible for you and God to have an open two-way conversation. My conversation happened because I created the atmosphere where I was preparing my mind and spirit to receive an answer. This was another step on my pursuit of peace.

Thinking takes practice. Do not confuse worrying with thinking. Worrying means fretting about something that hasn't happened yet. Thinking means concentrating on a solution that hasn't happened yet.

If you choose to think things through, you can even change what worries you. The words you use will actually control your thinking. New thoughts will reshape you. Thinking, combined with faith, will put you on the path of peace.

God invented peace. Peace is free to anyone who wants to partake. I agree with Billy Graham who writes, "It is possible to lead a God-guided, God-directed life."

Remember, it is true that a person becomes what he or she thinks about all day long.

A Fishing Story Example

Whom do you let into your boat?

It's really easy to look on the gloomy side of every situation and use non-positive words. It's easy to get sucked into someone else's negativity. It's easy to take on and attract their stress. You can even infect others with your own stress. The people you hang around with, will determine your level of stress. Stress loves company.

It is possible to repel stress by thinking peaceful thoughts! To make progress, you have to believe this statement.

I encourage you to begin thinking about the positive choices you have under your control. Begin deliberately choosing the people and good friends you want included in your boat. Begin today to build your own self-confidence and significance. How will you know when you are making progress?

Your friends will start seeking you out to help them with their problems. Believe it or not, you can even begin teaching others the skills of peace. It's called, "growing."

Mike heard me express In a Bible study group, "Be careful who you let in your boat." For some reason, that phrase took root in his emotions. He began changing his outlook on doing business. Mike was an advertising consultant. He started removing the clients who caused him grief and started replacing them with, "easy-to-get-along-with" clients. Mike's outlook on life shifted to optimism, hope, and enjoyment. He began to experience peace and a more successful life.

You can achieve anything if you surround yourself with good friends.

Starting Over

In a book was a story.

An energetic young man and an experienced old wise man were conspiring to keep the secret of success to themselves. They were both selfish and self-serving. Neither wanted to share their secrets. The younger man asked the old wise man where to hide their newly-found secrets of success.

The old wise man replied, "Let's hide them inside the man. He will never think of looking for them there."

I encourage you, when you don't know which way to turn, stop!

Pray to God. Backtrack to the wrong goals that have led you down the wrong roads. Cease pursuing those wrong goals and start shadowing paths of peace.

Peaceful friends help each other. You can use good friends to help you build a peace portfolio. I think you will also find that peaceful friends are not selfish like the young man and the old wise man above.

I suggest concentrating on happy things. It's OK to be happy! I suggest starting anew with new inspiration.

"I know that most folks can't comprehend the fact that I deliberately take the time to be peaceful. Most people will probably wonder why in the world I pray as I drive.

Most folks probably won't understand that, in my Jeep, I play good old Christian music, both bluegrass and classical orchestra. When I'm driving back and forth to my destination, I'm planting seeds of tranquility and peace. I have learned that a retreat for peace is valuable time invested."

If you find yourself in a situation caused by stress, it's OK to turn around and start over!

If you don't know what your own peace principles are, or more specifically, what you want your peace principles to be, you need not begin.

Happy?

Who decides if you are happy or unhappy? Your wife? Your husband? A loved one? Your son or daughter? Your boss? Your teacher? Your friends. The real estate market? The newspaper? The TV talk show hosts?

The answer is, "None of the above!"

"You" are the only person who can decide to make you happy. Peace is not something that just accidentally happens to you. Peace is a choice you proactively make.

When is the best time to start over to be happy? Any time. "Now" is very good. Yesterday is already gone.

Strange as the concept may seem to you, "Life is not about money." Whether you have little money or a lot of money, you have a choice to spend it on the "free" things of life. The free and valuable things of life are: love, beauty, appreciation, peace, friendship, caring, family time, breathing, walking, and listening to nature, God, and music.

I am happy because I trust in God on a daily basis. I choose to not worry. I choose not to stress out.

Outcome Thinking

Do you believe there is power in the written word? If you want results, write a letter using outcome thinking.

Before you start your letter, ask yourself, what do you want the outcome to be?

When your life is on the line, I think you will agree with me. The only things that truly matter are your health, your family and loved ones, and your state of mind. Everything that is valuable, comes to you free. Your being able to breathe, think, talk, eat, feel, and an internal knowledge of God, all come to you free, when you were born.

When you choose peace as the outcome, everyone wins.

Begin sharing your victories. As a peaceful effort, no matter how insignificant the victories may seem at the time, try writing down and recording the victories. You will start harvesting full grown thoughts of peace. Peace, in return, will help you cultivate more fields of positive peaceful thinking.

Surviving Debt

Begin with a new personal financial philosophy.

Dave Ramsey says, "Cut up your credit cards!" I agree.

I used to try to solve all my increasing expenses by charging more and more on my credit cards. I found that this pattern of using credit cards will lead to bankruptcy faster than any other financial tactic.

I actually experienced bankruptcy because I wouldn't face facts.

My friend, Larry, told me, "I don't care how many graphs you make on your computer, it still doesn't change the fact that you still aren't making enough money!"

He then added, "You are already bankrupt. You just haven't declared it yet."

I felt dejected, dismal, and down in the dumps. My part time job had just been eliminated. I had no money. I barely scraped by. I couldn't handle working any more. At the Court House, on the bankruptcy day, my lawyer asked, right there, on the spot, for the payment of the balance of his fee. I didn't know what to tell him. I told him that, "I really am a bankrupt person." I wrote out the check. I had $20.00 left in my checkbook. My old 1987 Jeep had a half tank of gas.

I had just been through an unexpected divorce. The divorce court required me to pay monthly support to my ex-wife. I lived on credit card debt for over a year. In the divorce, I received all the previous joint debt. I was on a collision course to crash and burn. The bankruptcy decision overtook my life.

I discovered that it is not possible to drop out of this world without still having to earn money. My friends gave me the encouragement to begin again. Only this time, I said, "If I have to work, and there is really no other choice, I'm going to do something I enjoy."

In my desperation attempts to find peace, I started going fishing with my friend, every month, for a week at a time. Overall, my self-esteem was still at the bottom.

I worked all the time. Very gradually I started my slow-down journey towards peace. I always believed that I was the income generator and provider for my family. No one could ever accuse me of not working hard. The reward, however, was a divorce, bankruptcy, and a double bypass heart operation.

Hopefully you will recognize the encouragement I'm suggesting to you. As soon as possible, immediately begin changing your income structure so that the outgo is less than the income. As you rid yourself of monthly bills, the relief you feel will help calm you down. By decreasing your spending habits, your entire being will begin to experience unruffled serenity.

You will be like I was. When all the credit card bills were completely gone, I experienced a peace that surpassed all understanding.

This story put life into perspective for me.

There was a story about a ten-year-old boy. His thirteen-year-old sister had a life-threatening illness and desperately needed a blood transfusion. Her illness required a blood transfusion of the same type from a family member. The boy was the only one in the family who had the correct blood type antibodies.

When the doctor explained the situation to the boy, he thought about it for a while, and then said, "Ok. I'll do it."

Later as the little boy was lying on the gurney beside his sister, while the transfusion was taking place, he asked the doctor, "Doctor, now when do I die?"

The doctor immediately reassured him and replied, "Oh no, son, you aren't going to die."

You see the little boy thought he was giving all of his blood to his sister. Who is the rich person in this story?

Mr. Peace

My youngest daughter called me on the phone a few years back, and asked to speak to, "Mr. Peace."

"That's me," I replied.

"I have rebounded from defeat and setbacks. I have found that sharing my faith helps encourage others."

"I now throw off the shackles of my old life. My new life consists of being happy, having fun, with less and less worry.

"I already know many things that don't work. I now allow myself to think clearly. I can take things in life as they come. I can live a rejoicing 'overcoming obstacles' life."

"I forgive myself."

"Now I can open my mind to creativity and clear thinking. Whatever comes my way, I face it with a grin."

Here are some more peace principles that changed my life.

Accomplishments 1996

- Went fishing more often than before.
- Dropped all my expenses to minimum
- Spent more time with my kids and grandkids

- Developed better ways of dealing with conflict
- Overall happier
- Hooked into the biggest fishes ever
- Learned how to play my guitar better
- Photo album of memories completed
- Learned how to fly fish
- Lost 7 pounds from March through December
- I got my ankle healed up so it doesn't bother me
- Read my part of the Bible almost 4 times through
- Read "Day by Day with Billy Graham" almost 5 times
- Read "The Power of Positive Thinking" by Norman Vincent Peale 8 times

Zig Ziglar, a nationally known motivational speaker said, "God can mend your broken heart... provided you give God all the pieces."

Matthew 6:26
"Look at the birds of the air; they do not sow or reap or stow away in barns, and yet your heavenly Father feeds them. Are you not much more valuable than they? Who of you by worrying can add a single hour to his life?"

Ecclesiastes 6: 14
"When times are good, be happy; but when times are bad, consider: God has made the one as well as the other. Therefore a man cannot discover anything about his future."

My Story

During my initial formative years as a loyal and dedicated hard worker, the grocery business provided a dependable income. There were no real challenges other than to seek ways to get along with the many managers above me. The promise of a promotion sometime in the future... was always the guiding light.

I knew nothing of life. The challenges of longevity with my job kept me always pursuing the only goal I ever had at that time ... to be promoted to a manager with more income. There were no more aspirations for me. I worked for almost 18 years in the grocery business chasing that dream.

I entered the realm of real estate sales. The freedom to work as hard as I wanted, helped me increase my income. I now had free control of my time with the "ever-present" possibility of a higher income. The real estate sales career overtook all my life decisions.

I now had freedom to work when I wanted, as hard as I wanted, and was paid accordingly. Later, when the real estate career faltered, income and life became more difficult. At that time, I am sure that I wasn't concerned about finding peace.

Living on commission was always an ever-present problem. I figured that hard work and spending more and more time with clients would help me achieve the goal of providing for my family. I was wrong!

[32]

One day, the issue of time came into vivid focus for me. My oldest daughter came to me and wanted help with getting her driver's license! I suddenly realized that I had let all that precious growing-up time pass me by! The same was true of my youngest daughter who was two years younger.

Yes, at night, early on, I tucked my daughters into bed and said prayers with them. But my mind and time was always occupied with work and making money, making enough money to get by on... and sometimes go to Hawaii on vacation.

When I realized that time with my daughters had slipped into oblivion, I began making course corrections. I began scheduling around family events.

I discovered that hard work was not the answer to life.

I kept the stress to myself, thinking that the results of my labor were the most important.

Then I began to change and to purposely make my life more meaningful. I uncovered the fact that there is no turning back on a valuable family life.

Then came the divorce! I was shocked beyond despair.

I believed that I would always be the good guy.

"Divorce" was never a consideration for me. All I ever wanted was for my wife to stay at home and raise the kids.

I finally got to the point that I couldn't handle any kind of stress. I kept all my problems inside of me. I didn't confide with anyone, not even with my wife. I never really knew how to communicate with her. I was stubborn, always thinking I could work my own way out of problems.

Over time, after going through ten years of a consistently bad real estate market, and eventually a divorce, my problems surfaced everywhere. Bankruptcy happened. Then I had a double bypass heart operation.

I packed up all my things into my small Honda, and moved to Las Vegas to get my Nevada Real Estate Broker's license and start over somewhere else. I tried to regain some sense in my life. I was running out of money.

It was December right after Christmas. I sat on a cold cement bench, peeling an orange. I was praying.

Suddenly, a voice from over my left shoulder said, "You have to go back." It was a real voice that I heard.

I repacked my Honda, and returned to Colorado. With no money and no prospects of a job, I had to come to grips with my situation. How am I going to get by? How do I make a comeback?

I have described my life this way.

My life was a shambles. I felt as flat as a pancake. I felt hurt. I was a failure. I went through the divorce, bankruptcy, and the heart operation. I had no self-worth. I didn't know which way to turn or jump. I couldn't make decisions on my own. I couldn't face reality. I felt miserable. In fact I was so miserable, I didn't know I was miserable.

I asked myself, "What's the use of working? What am I working for?"

My answer was one of frustration, defeat, and anger.

"You know what, I really don't care anymore."

That's what I was telling myself.

My journey has led me on a path of peace that I never expected to happen. You can experience that path of peace, too.

Maybe you need a "baseball bat up the side of your head" to begin making well-chosen outcomes.

Maybe it's just a gentle nudge from a friend, pastor, or confidant, or a nudge from a book like you are reading right now.

Maybe you have to begin truly "believing" for the first time.

A gentle prayer can catapult you into freedom you have never had before.

A memorized Bible verse can become your first step on the path to peace.

It's funny how God works. He usually doesn't tell you exactly what to do. He always leaves you suspended, with a decision to make. That's always the hard part, taking the time to make a decision, not knowing what the outcome will be. I guess that's called faith.

I like my life. I enjoy time off. I like my freedom to do and to pursue the important things in life. I like the peace I'm developing. I like leading a God directed life (a God Guided life.)

A real estate sales trainer and speaker told a story illustrating how to encourage a buyer to make a decision about buying a house. He told the story of a man who was sitting on a fence.

A passer-by stopped and asked the man, "How long have you been sittin' on that fence?"

"Long, long time," replied the man.

"How come?"

"Well, I can't make a decision on which way to jump."

The passer-by thought for a moment and then replied, "If you go ahead and jump, you will find out sooner!"

Do you really want to do something that makes you feel good and genuinely peaceful right away?

Anonymously, pay $10.00 towards a stranger's breakfast.

Find five good friends. Good friends will help you have the right attitude towards life. The friends you choose determine whether you win or lose. It has been said that, "A good friend is someone who knows all about you, but still likes you anyway." If they are lucky, most folks only have one or two good friends. Set a goal to have at least five good friends.

Peace principle: You become what you think about all day long.

Proverbs 16:3
"Commit to the Lord whatever you do, and your plans will succeed."

Psalm 29:11
"The Lord gives strength to his people; the Lord blesses his people with Peace."

Isaiah 26:3
"You will keep him in perfect peace him whose mind is steadfast, because he trusts in you. Trust in the Lord forever, for the Lord, the Lord is the rock eternal."

Peace Journey

No matter how much money you have, you can't buy peace. No matter how much money you have, you can't buy an abundant life.

To start your peace journey, try writing down a personal "Yearly Accomplishment List." Start with the little accomplishments. Try summarizing your accomplishments for each month. Then list the yearly accomplishments.

You will find that when you start on the path following God, you get to experience peace, free of charge. You receive a new feeling of truth coming into existence. That new feeling becomes prominent in every activity you undertake. Peace and freedom join hands when you walk on the path of peace.

You will simply find a more rewarding way to live. Have courage. Develop true faith.

Suggestion: read Bible verses every morning, memorizing the verses that apply directly to you. Underline those verses for easy reference. I suggest you also read ten daily bible devotions every morning. Take time to regularly read good books. Take time to pray every day.

If an automobile tire isn't in balance, it wears out very quickly. If it isn't continually recharged, a car battery eventually runs out of power. If a car runs out of gas, it will stop in the middle of nowhere, or worse, in tangling traffic. If the oil isn't checked and filled regularly, the car engine will seize up.

Similarly, the human body is in constant need of tuning for proper balanced performance. The same is especially true of the human heart. If there is no room allowed for peace, sooner or later, the body will break down into a heart attack. That's the factual outcome of stress.

Find a park or a lake and make a friend with the quiet time. When you slow down, peace can knock at your door. When you begin taking time to set worthwhile priorities, peace can easily walk in.

Bottom line is that you do have the ability and the right to peace. You have the power of choice to make your life different... and better.

"Stress removal is like garbage removal. It has to be done at least once every week, or every day. The garbage truck comes through my alley very early in the morning, before most people are waking up. It makes an extremely rank roar of grinding, engine grumbling, and banging around. I'm sure the removal process can't afford to get behind schedule. Peace comes from knowing that the noise of stress is always short-lived and temporary."

Consider that it's time to replace some of your stress thoughts you may have harbored for a long time.

Replace "no time" with "slow down." Replace "worry" with "peace." Replace "mistake" with "next time." Replace "push harder" with "think more."

"Remove All Stress From My Life."

This goal was so simply stated and powerful that it literally came true! You will discover that having fun and laughing is far more important than being wise and worrying. You can start over. You can start anew.

Start afresh with new goals.

Goals don't always have to be money or advancement centered.

For example, I wanted to be, "The greatest Papa (grandpa) around. I actually achieved that goal four years later. Both my daughters told me, within a few months of each other, "Dad, you are the greatest Papa ever."

"Around this house you eat, sleep, and play the piano!"

Early on, this was the admonition my two daughters received from their mother. That basic guideline continued down the generations, from both my daughters and all the way to my five grandkids. All still play the piano.

"Singin' for the Lord," was the title of the CD my youngest daughter created. She taught her three boys to sing in three part harmony while she played the songs on the piano as accompaniment. I helped by learning how to reproduce the CDs for her.

Peace is a very simple principle that many people never grasp or understand. Peace comes from trusting and believing in God, Jesus, prayer, and the Bible.

A verse in the Bible that has always encouraged me is, "The truth shall set you free!"

Peace is only a short journey away for you. Start to experience truth and open your mind to peace.

When you are being pursued by a line of cars as you go up or down a mountain road, pull over and let the cars and trucks go by.

Bottom line for the pursuit of peace is this. The only true peace comes from God as a free gift. Jesus tells us in John, Chapter 14, that He is the giver of peace. Our action step is to receive that peace.

"Peace I leave with you; My peace I give to you; not as the world gives do I give to you. Do not let your heart be troubled, nor let it be fearful. John 14:27 NASU

My anchor Bible verse for peace is this verse from Philippians 4. I recommend that everyone who struggles with finding peace, is to memorize this verse. No matter what the situation, I fall back on the instructions given here.

Philippians 4:6-7 NASU
Be anxious for nothing, but in everything by prayer
and supplication, with thanksgiving, let your requests
be made known to God. And the peace of God, which
surpasses all comprehension, will guard your hearts
and your minds in Christ Jesus.

The above verse can be broken down into two parts, our part and God's part.

Our part:

In everything by prayer and supplication, with thanksgiving, make our requests known to God.

God's part:

God gives us the peace of God which surpasses all comprehension.

God will guard our hearts and minds in Christ Jesus.

This is my "go to" verse in my darkest hours when I am facing heart surgery, money problems, experiencing the loss of a friend or a family member or facing the black hole of depression.

I've given you lots of techniques and things to do to help you pursue peace, and they have helped me stay peaceful, but in the end, to acquire peace, you must receive the peace from God that comes only as a free gift.

I finish off these peace principles with a letter I recently received from a good friend of mine. In times past, he could not have written this letter of encouragement. He was definitely too stressed out back then. We have been through a lot together. We have helped each other through all the major difficulties in life. We are best friends.

> *Ron*
> *After meeting with you for coffee, it was clear to me that the Great Encourager could use some reciprocation. You have received more than your share of bad news recently. You are experiencing something I am very familiar with, depression. I know what an awful grip it has and how it colors our every thought and word. It can make you look at your life's passion of spreading the word of God and encouraging others as being nor not. I am but just one of many that you have encouraged when they were facing tough times. Your faith always got you and your friends through hard times together. I wanted you to know how much your encouragement meant to me all those years that I struggled with my demons. I am a much calmer person now. You taught me how important it is to seek peace and I thank you for it.*
>
> *I am going to encourage you and oddly, myself, to do those things that bring us peace. I think you are right to say that you are not going to worry about money. In the end, it just does not matter. What does matter is that you hang onto all of the good you have done and all the wonderful differences that you have encouraged in the lives of others. I*

believe those experiences are truly the treasures that you possess.

I want you to focus on those blessings that you do have and not waste any more precious time fretting over money. The stuff is ultimately worthless as far as God is concerned. NO MORE WORRIES. You have a nice comfortable place to live and many friends that will pitch in to help you. We both need to redesign our lives seeking those things that bring us energy, and staying away from those things that do not.

You have been living a life of peace, mostly retired, following your desires. You have figured out how to trade very few hours for dollars. It seems to me that you have accomplished your goal of living a peaceful life. That does not need to change. If anything, it is time to recommit to it, rise above it, and relish the fact you know what things in life are actually of value.

Have a Blessed Day!
ML

Other books by Ron Camerrer
Log Cabin Miracles

This is a story of how an old man and a teenager struggle to live together. The teenager has the unexpected opportunity to learn about peace, bluegrass gospel music, and respect. It's how the teenager's miracle turnaround is molded by his environment, God, and friendship.

Old and young generations, even separated by years, can work together. It is about the miracle of giving.

Log Cabin Miracles is available on Amazon.com

Other books by Ron Camerrer
Guitar Miracles

Author Ron Camerrer brings to life how even the smallest prayers achieve great results. Ron uses the guitar as the central theme to convey the message. Sam's acquisition of a guitar helps the teen group to be inspired and begin performing. This is a story about Sam's beginning to have belief in God. It's an awakening 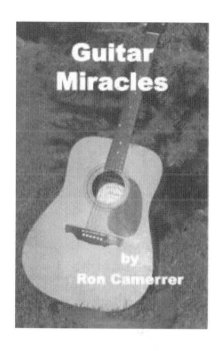 process for a new believer to positively change his thinking, even if he has never known or thought about God before. Sam's faith and new belief is established by inspiration through song- and his guitar.

Guitar Miracles is available on Amazon.com

Other books by Ron Camerrer
PAPA'S Stories

Written for his family, this collection of "Papa's Stories" is a glimpse into that process of remembering. Some of the stories are just for fun reading. Others are about some of the challenges Ron encountered through the years. He shares his victories, failures, and his journey to follow God's leading.

PAPA'S Stories

By Ron Camerrer

Ron has two daughters and five grandkids. They call him "Papa."

Ron made a decision to, "Become the greatest Grandpa ever!" He proceeded to spend as much time as possible with his two daughters and five grandkids. He wrote down these true stories so that his legacy may remain for future generations. This book will inspire you to record your own stories for your family.

Papa's Stories is available on Amazon.com

Other books by Ron Camerrer
Bluegrass Gospel Jams

Do you have a song in your heart and a tap in your toe?

This is a "how-to" book that encourages Bluegrass Gospel music lovers everywhere. This book provides valuable insight for everyone; lovers of bluegrass music, musicians, want-to-be musicians, and jam leaders.

Ron shares key aspects of music, fun, and real life ministry.

Learn of his passion to have everyone *"participate"* - *"not perform"*- in a Bluegrass Gospel Jam event.

Bluegrass Gospel Jams is available on Amazon.com

About the Author

Ron Camerrer, a Colorado native since 1956, loves to encourage others. Retired and living in Fort Collins, Colorado, Ron spends his time writing, fishing, and encouraging others over a cup of coffee. His real passion is helping people find peace in today's stressful world.

To receive daily verses of peace, to request volume quantities of books, or to discuss the pursuit of peace in your life, please email Ron at Ron@pursuitofpeace.net

66417647R00031

Made in the USA
Middletown, DE
06 September 2019